Overcoming Laziness

Discover How to Stop Being Lazy and Get Things Done!

by Gretchen Pilar

Table of Contents

Introduction 1

Chapter 1: Understanding the Roadblocks to Productivity 7

Chapter 2: Creating a Well-Thought-Out Plan 17

Chapter 3: Mastering the Art of Time Management 23

Chapter 4: How to Motivate Yourself 31

Chapter 5: Putting Yourself in the Right Environment 35

Conclusion 39

Introduction

People get lazy all the time. If you stop and think about the times you've decided not to do something productive or to put something off that could have been accomplished at that very moment, you'd realize how much time you actually waste in a single day. Take a look at the bigger picture and you'll realize how much time you've actually wasted in your entire life. The older you are, the harsher this reality becomes.

Needless to say, the prime characteristic of the most successful and productive people is that they're **not** lazy, so if you want to become more successful and productive in life - and thus happier too - then tackling laziness is a great place to start. Men and women of success hardly ever put off anything until later if it could be done today, and they always work more efficiently than most people, accomplishing more than the average person would in a given period of time.

A person is considered lazy when he or she basically refuses to do something that should be done — may it be for work, school, or even for fun (i.e. planning that camping trip for your family). They're basically setting aside their potential to be productive, settling for what they feel like doing at the moment instead. While taking a load off every now and then is perfectly healthy in terms of decompressing and relaxing, it becomes a bad thing when "taking it easy" becomes a common excuse to procrastinate, especially when you are no longer aware you're even doing it because you have been so accustomed to the habit of laziness.

Laziness is actually caused by a number of factors, ranging from trivial to significant. Some people become overwhelmed by the task in front of them and therefore get discouraged, while others become too complacent or don't understand the gravity of their responsibilities. Hence, the procrastination.

This isn't just about getting something done though. It's actually about being able to make the most of your time and abilities. Whether you're a person who can focus on only one thing at a time, or you're the type who prefers to multi-task, you become lazy when you don't do as much as you know you can. Overcoming laziness, therefore, is all about maximizing productivity, which all starts with the resolve to make the most of every day.

In this book, you will learn how to get past those moments of passivity by understanding how they happen and what you can do to overcome them. This means learning about the most basic obstacles to productivity and knowing how to deal with them and manage yourself so that you are able to make the most of your schedule and stick to whatever plan you make. After all, being able to successfully accomplish a plan you came up with yourself will encourage you to accomplish what you set out to on a regular basis in the future. You will also learn how to channel that sense of productivity onto other people. Chances are, you also need them to be less lazy as well.

It's going to take a lot of work and a willingness to make some simple lifestyle changes. But the moment you start reaping the benefits of being a productive individual, you will realize that it's worth it in the end.

© Copyright 2015 by Miafn LLC - All rights reserved.

This document is geared towards providing reliable information in regards to the topic and issue covered. The publication is sold with the idea that the publisher is not required to render accounting, officially permitted, or otherwise, qualified services. If advice is necessary, legal or professional, a practiced individual in the profession should be ordered.

- From a Declaration of Principles which was accepted and approved equally by a Committee of the American Bar Association and a Committee of Publishers and Associations.

In no way is it legal to reproduce, duplicate, or transmit any part of this document in either electronic means or in printed format. Recording of this publication is strictly prohibited and any storage of this document is not allowed unless with written permission from the publisher. All rights reserved.

The information provided herein is stated to be truthful and consistent, in that any liability, in terms of inattention or otherwise, by any usage or abuse of any policies, processes, or directions contained within is solely and completely the responsibility of the recipient reader. Under no circumstances will any legal responsibility or blame be held against the publisher for any reparation, damages, or monetary loss due to the information herein, either directly or indirectly.

Respective authors own all copyrights not held by the publisher.

The information herein is offered for informational purposes solely, and is universal as so. The presentation of the information is without contract or any type of guarantee assurance.

The trademarks that are used are without any consent, and the publication of the trademark is without permission or backing by the trademark owner. All trademarks and brands within this book are for clarifying purposes only and are the owned by the owners themselves, not affiliated with this document.

Chapter 1: Understanding the Roadblocks to Productivity

There's an old saying: it's the little things that count. As far as what makes you lazy is concerned, that saying is a golden truth. While most people will consider it a feeling, laziness does not pop out of nowhere. There is always a reason why you are not on your feet with what you're meant to be doing at the moment. Some of these causes are pretty tangible and easy to understand, while others seem very vague, to the point that we'd dismiss them as harmless.

Remember that being lazy doesn't always have to come in the form of you lying around doing nothing (although that's always a very good example). Rather, it happens every time you end up not doing something you should. Here are some of the common scenarios and possible solutions to when you find yourself more or less unwilling to do something at the moment (even when you very well know you should).

You can't seem to get out of bed. Many times people find themselves unwilling to get out of bed. You wake up at whatever time in the morning, and you still feel like rolling around your bed, and this is usually for varying reasons.

More often than not, this is a problem of lack of motivation. Yes, some people need to be given a good reason to get out of bed and start the day. For some people, especially the morning people, this occurs naturally, while others find it a rare occurrence. For example, even though you are the type of person who lingers in bed, there will be mornings when you suddenly jump out of bed because of something exciting or urgent, such as when you realize you're late for class or it's that day when you and your friends are going out on a road trip, or when you hear a loud noise outside your house. Whatever the cause, the point is, you're up, and it will take an exceptionally lazy person to actually get back to bed and sleep again.

Getting out of bed therefore requires a concrete reason to do so. If you don't have one that occurs regularly, you create the conditions that will. Here are some things you can try, for starters:

- Set up your room in such a way that enough sunlight gets in when morning comes. Make sure not to close all the curtains so that your room doesn't appear dark in the morning.

- Set an alarm clock. There are also mobile apps that feature alarm clocks with "anti-snooze" features so that they're not easy to switch off when they ring.

- Set the timer on your air-conditioning. The change in temperature will encourage your body to awake.

- Have some water available beside your bed. Drinking a glass in the morning might be what you need to finally wake up.

- Try stretching even when you're lying down. People who sleep in normally maintain a curled up or stationary position.

You'll notice that these are ways to give your body that much needed "push" to finally snap out of the state of sleepiness. They're essentially stop-gap measures. But once your body gets accustomed to the feeling of being awake during a specific time in the morning, it will become a habit, and your days will start to begin early.

Your body lacks energy. It's possible that you don't get out of bed easily because you lack sleep as well, but not getting the right amount of sleep affects you throughout the day. Sometimes you also don't feel like doing anything because you're hungry or really thirsty and you don't even realize it.

Your body is the first piece of capital for being productive. As such, you should never take your own health for granted. Some people unknowingly skip meals or miss sleep just to get some work done, but what they don't realize is that a healthy and fully energized body will give them what they need to make sure that more work gets done fast without necessarily doing overtime.

When you feel lazy or unmotivated, it's important to check if you've eaten or had enough rest recently. Maybe it's time for you to have a meal or have a power nap. If so, it'll be easy to get back to work after. In fact, having coffee and some snacks while you work is a good way to maintain the level of energy you have while working. Just be careful not to make a mess of your workspace.

Something is bothering you. We all encounter emergencies that need our immediate attention, but sometimes we get worked up about sudden news or occurrences that don't really need to be prioritized at the moment. On the one hand, they could be things that are indeed important, but you can't really do much about at the time, such as when you heard that your friend was rushed to the hospital that morning or when you receive an email about some debts being overdue. On the other hand, they could actually be things that just tend to occupy your focus for a long time, such as when you have a fight with your partner, or when someone who promised to call you hadn't contacted you yet.

Your brain will naturally gravitate towards these nagging thoughts and end up focusing on them unnecessarily. These problems will eventually drain you mentally because you've been thinking about them too much, and emotionally because you've been worrying about them. This results in you not getting anything done at all.

To deal with these problems, you need to assess the things that interrupt your regular schedule. The real emergencies are those that can be dealt with at the moment. But if you are faced with problems that you don't have the power to solve, then maybe you need to deal with them later even when it seems like the most important thing to do at the moment is to wallow in that situation. Moreover, if the problem is something that turns out to be trivial, you need to bring your attention back to what you're supposed to be doing.

The truth is, everyone has worries, but even worries have a proper place in your schedule.

You get distracted by something. People who work on computers with internet connections can easily experience this problem. They usually end up scrolling down their Facebook newsfeeds too much or start watching one too many videos on YouTube. When they realize they've wasted too much time, they forget where they were or what they were working on and eventually lose the motivation to continue working. They then end up taking a break they don't really deserve.

You can only break this terrible habit with discipline. If you must, find ways to limit your access to social media, or stay away from your laptop if you can work without it. Distractions can come in many forms as well, such as the people who pass by or the alerts you get on your phone. If you're supposed to be doing something, then you should be cutting off sources of distraction, with an exception to communication outlets that might be needed for emergencies.

Something breaks, or there is a problem. Too often we use technical problems as an excuse to stop working and we don't even realize it. When, for example, we are used to working with a computer or some kind of staple material, we often lose the drive to work when the company laptop malfunctions or you run out of material. Instead of doing something about the problem (i.e. finding alternatives or fixing the problem at hand), we think that it's not our job to troubleshoot the issue and just wait for someone else to fix it before going back to work.

When this happens, you're basically just making excuses, which is another form of lazy. Keep in mind that no matter what happens, you still need to do your job or accomplish the task before you. If the problem is outside your control, find a way around it. In reality, it's rarely a technical or logistical problem that keeps anything from getting done. Rather, it's our unwillingness to find a way around that problem that does.

Now, the causes mentioned above are simply some of the common reasons why a person will get lazy. More likely than not, you won't even have noticed that these were the reasons why you've been slacking off, because all you will be feeling (and all the other people will notice) is the unwillingness to get anything done. That's exactly how a person gets lazy.

But if you are aware of the fact that laziness and procrastination has a root cause, you're able to deal with them as they come up, and you have less reason not to become productive.

Of course, preventing productivity roadblocks is just half the battle. Moving towards higher levels of productivity will not only banish laziness out of your system for good, but ultimately allow you to get more work done. That's what you need to learn next.

Chapter 2: Creating a Well-Thought-Out Plan

A lot of people really underestimate the power of a well thought out plan. You just don't know it, but the most successful people around actually have something cooked up in their heads. Some people are better at planning than others, but those who go places are usually the ones who know where they ought to go from the beginning. Sure, it may seem like that friend of yours who is succeeding in his career doesn't carry a planner or organizer around with him, but you can be sure he has organized his day, week, and even month in one way or another.

But planning isn't just some secret key to success. It's actually a powerful tool against laziness. When you spend a lot of time trying to figure out what to do when you wake up in the morning, you either waste a lot of time otherwise put to good use or you get exhausted and decide to procrastinate.

The art of planning is not something that's mastered overnight. But if all you want is to be able to overcome your laziness, then you just need a very basic tool: the to-do list.

Making That To-Do List

You always hear that old advice of writing stuff down on your phone or notebook, but there's a big chance you don't really get around to doing that, thinking that you'll be able to figure things out as you go along. But if you're reading this guide, chances are you don't always figure things out along the way, and you end up being lazy and unproductive. So why not actually try writing down the things you want to do?

There are many reasons why even the shortest list of things can help you get moving:

- **You avoid wasting time and motivation when you forget stuff.** Regardless of age or mental health, the reality is that we forget things. There's no shame in that, at least no more than the consequences of forgetting to do something really important. If you've had those weekdays where you feel like lounging around the house because it doesn't seem like you have much to do and then, when it's too late, you suddenly remember that you were actually supposed to be at some important meeting somewhere, then you know how forgetting stuff can make you lazy. The thing is, it's so easy not to forget something when you just write it down.

- **You already warm up your brain for what's ahead.** Planning itself can be time consuming, but this is significantly reduced to an efficient level when you separate the thinking process to a time frame different from the one where you should be executing the plan. The best time for this is when you're actively committing to these tasks (which is also the time when you should be writing them down on your list). Every time you jot down an item on that to-do list, you actually also end up thinking and visualizing what you're supposed to be doing to accomplish that, which you're going to end up writing down. Before you know it, you've conveniently set a basic framework for the task before you. And when you have something already laid down for you, it's less likely that you are daunted by the task, since most of the process has already been thought out.

- **To-do lists provide a sense of urgency.** Once you've finished your list for a certain time frame (expect to make more lists in the future), you get a good picture of how much work is cut out for you. That's when you say "ah, I've got this much to do within a certain period of time." And this kind of awareness is really important because much of laziness comes from complacency brought about by an illusion that you've got too much time on your hands. You've probably already experienced that rush you get in finishing a certain task because you know you've still got other stuff to do. A to-do list simulates that rush constantly.

- **It protects you from being burned out.** At some point you're going to need to be able to prioritize some tasks over the other. Having too much on your plate can also cause laziness, only this time it's in the form of being mentally paralyzed from the overwhelming number of things to do. Listing all the things you need to do will help you determine whether you're committing to way too many things. Later, you're going to learn how to pick the tasks that can be dealt with later or by other people.

Of course, you can take advanced steps to getting your tasks organized with planners, calendars, etc., but you can already do great things with a simple sheet of paper that lists all the things you need to do in a day. Just make a habit of writing them down and you're going to experience less downtime in the future.

Tip: Try to write your to-do list on paper rather than your tablet or phone. Studies have shown that the mechanical act of writing actually has cognitive benefits, making it easier to imprint in your brain stuff you've written down. Thus, when you write down a list, you're not just writing it down on paper, but you're also embedding it in your mind.

Chapter 3: Mastering the Art of Time Management

Time is a very unique resource. It's one thing that always seems to run but we never have enough of. That's why managing the time is also a very important skill that every productive person needs to learn.

Time, however, can also be an obstacle. The longer a person works, the more likely he or she is to get tired or exhausted. People get older through time, and some people change and even lose parts of who they are. That's why people change careers as time passes. Time also dictates our goals, such as when there are deadlines or urgent matters that need to be addressed.

This is why being able to take control of one's own time is a trait of the successful and more productive people. It takes proper planning and strategy in order for you not to get caught in bad timing that could possibly keep you from getting anything accomplished. In this chapter, we will take a look at two important aspects of time in relation to fighting laziness.

Your Body Clock

As far as your body is concerned, not all 24 hours of the day are equal. In fact, science has consistently shown that some people are at a work advantage simply because of the time of the day. That's why we've got the morning people and the night owls, both of which have their own set of arguments why one is more productive than the other.

The truth, however, just like all other differentiations in people, is that people just have their own strengths and weaknesses, and those who become more productive are those who are able to manage these to their advantage. People who are not only aware of their changing productivity levels throughout the day, but also know how to arrange their schedule to harmonize with that trend naturally end up accomplishing more.

Now, it's very easy to determine whether you are a morning person or a night person. More often than not, a person's busy schedule would have already led him or her to work through the day, and then notice what times of the day he or she is able to accomplish more. Naturally, those times of the day when you've felt more productive are those times when your body is most alert, able to do things you can't during your personal off peak hours.

The bigger challenge, however, is knowing what to do when you're at the prime of your day and how to make the most of when you're at your off peak moments. There has been a lot of discourse around this, but the simple rule is to save all your logical and analytical tasks for the peak hours (i.e. day for morning persons and evening for night owls), and then save those creative tasks for when you're off peak.

During your peak time, your brain is most active and that's when you're able to sort out information in your head. During this time, your brain is able to function efficiently such that you are less likely to be distracted and are able to understand the problems before you more easily. Studying, solving math problems, etc., therefore fall into this category.

On the other hand, you are more likely to be creative when your brain is not fully most logically inclined. Contrary to popular belief, you're not utterly useless when you're tired. In fact, that's when you're better able to create things out of your imagination because your brain tends to be less critical and, for lack of a better term, starts to wander off. This is why you are easily distracted when you're beginning to get tired. This would be the right time to formulate ideas for a project, write down new thoughts, or something similar because our brains are less likely to shoot them down for scrutiny of logic.

If you try doing things the other way around, you end up not coming up with better ideas during the peak hours and consistently getting distracted when you're already tired. That's when you start getting lazy, and do a poorer job than you otherwise could.

Budgeting Your Time

As mentioned already, time is also a limited resource. Hence, you can't just take on everything, promising you'll be able to accomplish all of them within the day. As opposed to the old saying, your will isn't the only thing that makes the way possible. You need time as well.

When you are overburdened with work, you tend to get discouraged by all of it and end up doing nothing at all. To remedy that, you simply need to lighten your load. Here are a couple of things that you can keep in mind so as not to feel overwhelmed:

- Always check if you have time to do something before you commit to it. You'll find that it's less damaging to you and to other people to just say no outright than to say yes now and then take it back later.

- A good method of juggling different tasks is to always balance the short and long term tasks. Of course, you will want to give attention to those tasks that need to be finished sooner (i.e. those with impending deadlines), but once you've got the opportunity to decide which task you should do first, make sure you space things out rationally. Those tasks that have farther deadlines but will require more time to accomplish should be partially done between those tasks that you can finish in one sitting.

- Take note of certain tasks you usually do and keep track of the average times you take to finish them. This knowledge will come in handy when estimating whether you have enough time to work on them all in a day.

- Make sure you only work for as much as eight hours in one day. The reason why labor laws across countries protect workers from working more than eight hours within a 24 hour period is because you need to divide your day to accommodate the three basic needs (i.e. eight hours each of work, sleep, and play). Some people tend to overwork themselves and have no time to play anymore or, worse, they don't sleep anymore.

On that note, it's very important to always get enough rest between 24 hour periods and make an allowance for breaks in between work hours. Managing time as discussed above will only be beneficial if your body gets enough rest regularly. Otherwise, there will be a blurred line between those peak and off peak hours, and you'll just be worn out across the board, and that's when you get really lazy.

Balance your time and your work load, however, and you'll be making the most of every day, and not feel like you're wasting your life.

Chapter 4: How to Motivate Yourself

Beating laziness is as much a mental battle as it is a logistical one. No matter how much we come up with a daily routine, no two days will ever be exactly the same. The results are likely to be similar, but we will always end up doing things differently each day. Some of these differences will be unnoticeable and inconsequential, but there will be those happenings that will throw us off course. When this happens, we end up not having any idea of what to do or where to start, and we get lazy.

Of course, a cup of coffee can perk you up, but that's not the only thing that can get you going when things feel a bit heavier than usual. Here are some natural pick-me-ups that can help when you need them.

- **Break down large tasks to smaller ones.** Big projects are daunting because of their size. To make them less intimidating, you can try looking at them on a milestone basis, looking at separate steps that require different methods. That way, not only are you able to focus on each step in detail, you're also able to space out the tasks into different time periods, thus allowing you to accomplish other tasks or take breaks in between.

- **Set deadlines for yourself.** Ever notice how we seem to work significantly faster when an essay or task is almost due? To most people, challenging yourself to finish a task within a particular period can emulate that sense of urgency. Some people even use timers on their computers to alert them as to how much time they have left, and then issue personal rewards or punishments, depending on whether they meet the deadline.

- **Figure out why you're doing something.** In other words, try to understand why a particular task is so important. Urgency is not just a matter of time. If you can remind yourself clearly why a certain job is very important and even be aware of the consequences if the task isn't done, has proven to be a great motivation for all kinds of people countless times.

- **Learn to love what you do.** People only get lazy when they work. Nobody ever gets lazy doing what they love to do. Of course, not everything is fun. For those tasks that don't provide much enjoyment, you might want to try figuring out if there are fun ways to accomplish your task. If all else fails, at least promise yourself a reward for a job well done. If you can't give yourself a reason to look forward to doing the task, then give yourself a reason to look forward to finishing it.

We all need that little push to beat those lazy spells. Not all of us have life coaches, though, so it's important to learn how to push ourselves, especially when we need it the most. Eventually, you'll be glad that you nudged yourself to get things done.

Chapter 5: Putting Yourself in the Right Environment

Ever wonder why you need to go to a different place to get a vacation? It's because some places are better to relax at than others. Conversely, we also find that there are places that are easier to work in than others. That's why your environment plays an important role in making sure you don't get lazy. Here are a couple of rules that you should keep in mind:

- **Never work in your bedroom or any place or relaxation.** The reason for this is that your body is supposed to respond to the mood of the environment accordingly. Being in a place where you sleep or relax will naturally prompt your body to take it easy. If you mix your work and sleep place, you will end up confusing yourself, which is bad in two ways: not only will it ruin your sleep pattern, but you'll also feel sleepy easily.

- **Work in a well-lit place.** Dim lighting doesn't just make you feel sleepy, but it can also strain your eyes in a way that stresses and burns you out faster. The best kind of lighting is always natural light, so try to have a work space where you can have lots of that. If you're a night owl, make sure you've got adequate lighting. Sometimes we have to work under less than optimal conditions, but never let yourself work with poor lighting when you don't have to.

- **Mind the people around you.** Depending on who they are, people can either be motivations or distractions. Sometimes you need to keep yourself away from people that you leisurely spend time with and stick with workmates in order to feel the push you need. Take note, however, that not all workmates are productive elements to the environment, and not all children will make you want to procrastinate and play. This is all a matter of observing which kinds of people normally allow you to get things done, and sticking with them.

As the old saying goes, "a place for everything, and everything in its place." Keep in mind that there is a place to work hard and there is a place to relax. You need to know which is which.

Conclusion

Don't expect to be productive every single day. You will have your off moments, but that doesn't mean you should let that get the best of you. Learning to fight laziness is a habit in itself, and mastering that habit means having more control over what you're able to accomplish within a time period, be it a day, week, month, or even year.

More than that, understanding and eventually fixing the root cause of your unproductivity also means that you get to make the most of your life. It means being able to take a rest and get up without having to regret putting off some tasks that are almost due. It means being able to play or have fun without worrying about backlog when you get back to work. Because you are able to work when you should, you are also able to play and rest when you need to.

In other words, overcoming laziness means you get to achieve the ultimate goal of work-life balance. In the end, that's what every person really wants.

Finally, I'd like to thank you for purchasing this book! If you enjoyed it or found it helpful, I'd greatly appreciate it if you'd take a moment to leave a review on Amazon. Thank you!

Made in the USA
Middletown, DE
27 November 2020